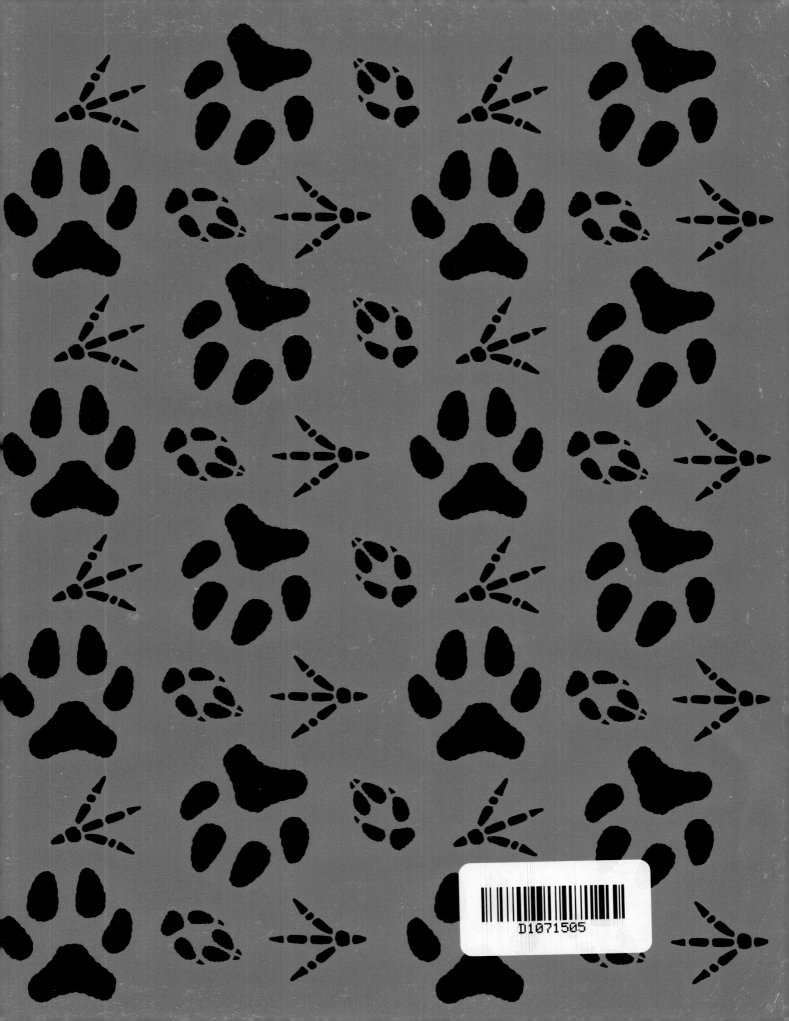

Hippopotamus
Page 8

A DORLING KINDERSLEY BOOK

Written and edited by
Jane Donnelly
Art Editor Sharon Grant
Assistant Editor David Nicoll
Deputy Managing Editor Dawn Sirett
Deputy Managing Art Editor
C. David Gillingwater
Production Katy Holmes
Picture Research Christine Rista
Photography Peter Anderson
and Frank Greenaway
Illustrators Ellis Nadler and
Derek Matthews
Consultant Juliet Clutton-Brock

First published in Great Britain in 1996
by Dorling Kindersley Limited,
9 Henrietta Street, London WC2E 8PS

Copyright © 1996 Dorling Kindersley Limited, London
Visit us on the World Wide Web at http://www.dk.com

A CIP catalogue record for this book
is available from the British Library.

ISBN: 0-7513-5464-3

Colour reproduction by Chromagraphics, Singapore
Printed and bound in Italy by L.E.G.O.

Dorling Kindersley would like to thank the following for
their kind permission to reproduce photographs:
t=top, b=bottom, c=centre, l=left, r=right

Bryan & Cherry Alexander 4cr, 16-17; **American Museum
of Natural History, New York** 15b; **Ardea, London** /
Adrian Warren 11tr; **BBC NHU** / Jeff Foott 4bl, 13 main;
Heather Angel 9t, 18tl; **Bruce Coleman** / John Concatosa 10tl;
Dr M P Kahl 6bl, 19tr; Dr Eckart Pott 12br; Hans Reinhard
20tl, 21tr; Leonard Lee Rue 17tr; Rinie Van Meurs 17cr;
NHPA / John Shaw 4cl, 12 main; **Planet Earth Pictures** /
Nick Greaves 4tl, 8-9b, Anup and Manoj Shah 7cr;
Tony Stone Images 13 tl, 15t; **Zefa** 5br, 8tl,14b.

Gorilla
Page 10

Walrus
Page 16

Scale
Look out for drawings
like this – they show
the size of the animals
compared with people.

Grizzly bear
Page 12

Moose
Page 13

MIGHTY
GIANTS
OF THE WILD

Giraffes
Page 18

Rhinoceros
Page 20

Whale
Page 14

Elephant
Page 6

DORLING KINDERSLEY
LONDON • NEW YORK • STUTTGART • MOSCOW

Elephant

The elephant is the largest animal on land. It is found in Asia and Africa. Females and calves live in a herd, while adult males live separately.

This African elephant is about 12 years old. It may live to be 70.

Handy nose
An elephant puts food and water into its mouth using its trunk. It's like a hand and nose in one!

Scale

At up to 1.5 metres long, a trunk is more than 30 times longer than your nose.

Baby elephants and some other baby mammals are called **calves**.

Thick, wrinkly skin traps moisture to keep the elephant cool.

AMAZING FACTS

African elephants have much larger ears than Asian elephants. An African elephant's ear flap can be 1.5 metres from top to bottom – as big as a blanket.

Baby elephants weigh 100-120 kg when they are born – that's more than a fully-grown human.

Just as humans are left- or right-handed, elephants use one tusk more than the other.

Elephants communicate with each other by using low, grumbling sounds that humans can't hear.

Two of a kind

There are two types of elephant: the Asian elephant and the larger African elephant. An adult male African elephant can weigh up to 5.4 tonnes.

Cushioned feet mean elephants can move quietly despite their size.

Tusks are long teeth that can be used as tools or weapons.

Hippopotamus

AMAZING FACTS

🐾 A male hippo's tusks can grow more than 50 cm long including the root – that's as long as your arm.

🐾 The hippo is the third largest animal on land. It weighs 2.5 tonnes. Its head alone can weigh 1 tonne.

🐾 A hippo's stomach is so big it can hold more liquid than a car's petrol tank! A hippo can't drink this much in one go, but it does eat more than 40 kg of food every day.

At more than three metres from head to tail, the huge hippopotamus is as long as a family-sized car. Hippos live in Africa, grazing at night alongside rivers. They spend the daytime keeping cool in water.

Scale

A hippo's skin produces special "pink sweat" that protects it from the sun.

Feathered friend

The bird sitting on this hippo is an oxpecker. Oxpeckers eat leeches and other parasites in a hippo's skin.

Hippos only have hair on their muzzles, in their ears, and at the tips of their tails.

🐾 Feeding on growing grass is called **grazing**. 🐾

Water babies

During the day, hippos like to be in water. They can hold their breath underwater for nearly five minutes.

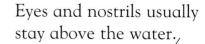

Eyes and nostrils usually stay above the water.

Oxpecker

Parasites live on or in other living things. They can be animals or plants.

Gorilla

Yawning warning

Gorillas are peaceful plant-eaters, but will bare their sharp canines to frighten off an enemy.

AMAZING FACTS

A fully-grown male gorilla can weigh up to 200 kg – that's more than two grown men.

Young gorillas sleep in nests they make in trees. Grown-up gorillas are too heavy and have to sleep on the ground.

Despite its impressive size, the most powerful of the apes is really a gentle giant. Gorillas live in family groups and only attack if they are threatened by another animal or gorilla.

Silvery grey hair on back

Great ape
The largest male gorilla protects the whole family group. These big males are called "silverbacks" because of the hair on their backs that turns silvery grey when they are about 12 years old.

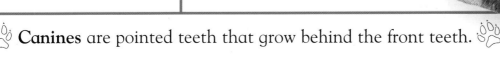

Family life
Up to 15 gorillas live together in a group. They travel through the rainforest, feeding on plants and shoots, and resting in nests.

Scale

Each gorilla has a unique noseprint.

Standing up can be a warning action as well as a way to reach food.

Upright stance
Standing on its hind legs, a male silverback can be up to 2 metres tall. Gorillas stretch up like this to reach for food. When they walk, they go slowly on all fours.

A gorilla's knuckles support its full weight as it walks.

A **noseprint** is the pattern of ridges on a gorilla's nose. 11

Grizzly bear

The North American grizzly bear is one of the largest bears, weighing up to 800 kg. This one is ready for a fight.

Scale

Thick, warm fur

Powerful jaws
Grizzly bears are omnivores. Their strong teeth and jaws can bite and chew through meat, shoots, and berries.

AMANG FACT
🐾 Grizzly bears are good at fishing. They catch fish from fast-running rivers using their mouths.

🐾 If an animal eats fruit and plants as well as meat, it is called an **omnivore**. 🐾

Moose

🐾 A moose's antlers can be 1.8 metres across. They are shed each winter and a new, larger pair grows each spring.

The largest deer in the world is the moose. A male can weigh more than 600 kg. Its antlers alone can weigh up to 30 kg. Moose live in North America, Europe, and Asia.

Scale

Antlers

Long legs allow a moose to stand in deep water to feed on river plants.

This long flap of skin is called a bell.

Head gear
A male uses its antlers to fight off other male rivals for a mate.

🐾 **Antlers** are outgrowths made of bone that grow on a deer's head. 🐾

Whales

There are more than 75 species of whale, ranging from giant blue whales to much smaller porpoises and dolphins. Although they look and swim like fish, whales are actually mammals.

Scale

Baleen plates

Grey whale
This whale only feeds in the summer. It lives off its own fat for the rest of the year.

Killer whale
Known for being ferocious hunters, killer whales eat porpoises, penguins, fish, and other sea creatures.

The dorsal, or back, fin can be as tall as a man.

Scale

Streamlined body helps the killer whale to swim at speeds of up to 65 km/h.

Baleen plates are brush-like fringes in a whale's mouth used for filtering food.

Flipper

Scale

Black and white
markings are unique
to each humpback
– just like we have
different faces.

Humpback whale
The humpback is
named after the hump
in front of its dorsal fin.
This whale has the largest
flippers of any whale.

Blue-grey colour gives
the whale its name.

At 25 metres long, this
whale is longer than
two buses.

Blue whale
This whale is the largest
animal in the world. It weighs
100 tonnes and can eat about
four tonnes of krill a day, which
is the weight of more than
14,000 potatoes.

Scale

Throat grooves
run down to belly.

Shrimp-like creatures, called **krill**, are a major part of the diet of many whales. 15

Walrus

The enormous walrus lives at the edge of the frozen polar ice in the Arctic ocean. A walrus may travel up to 3,000 km a year, following the movement of ice floes.

Scale

Powerful fighter
The walrus has only two enemies, the polar bear and the killer whale, but they rarely attack. The walrus is a strong opponent and can beat the polar bear in a fight.

Thick, protective skin

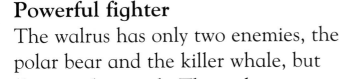

Ice floes are huge sheets of ice that float on the sea and drift with the currents.

Beach party

Hundreds of walruses sleep together in a huge pile like this, keeping each other warm. They have up to 10 cm of blubber under their skin to protect them from freezing temperatures.

A walrus's bristles are touch-sensitive and help it to find food such as shellfish.

Tusks can grow up to 55 cm long.

AMAZING FACTS

🐾 Walruses use their tusks to heave their huge bodies on to the ice and to scrape up shellfish from the seabed.

🐾 A walrus's skull is so thick that it acts like a crash helmet to protect the brain as the walrus breaks through ice.

🐾 Many animals that live in cold places have **blubber**, or fat, to keep them warm. 🐾 17

Giraffe

AMAZING FACTS

Despite its length, a giraffe's neck has only seven vertebrae – the same number as humans and all other mammals.

A male giraffe can be up to 6 metres tall – that's as high as a two-storey building.

Giraffes don't sleep much, but, when they do, some people think they rest like this, with their necks along their backs.

The graceful giraffe is the tallest animal in the world. It lives on the African grasslands. Giraffes use their long necks and flexible tongues to eat the leaves of tall trees.

Giraffes have between two and five small horns.

18 **Vertebrae** are neck and spine bones.

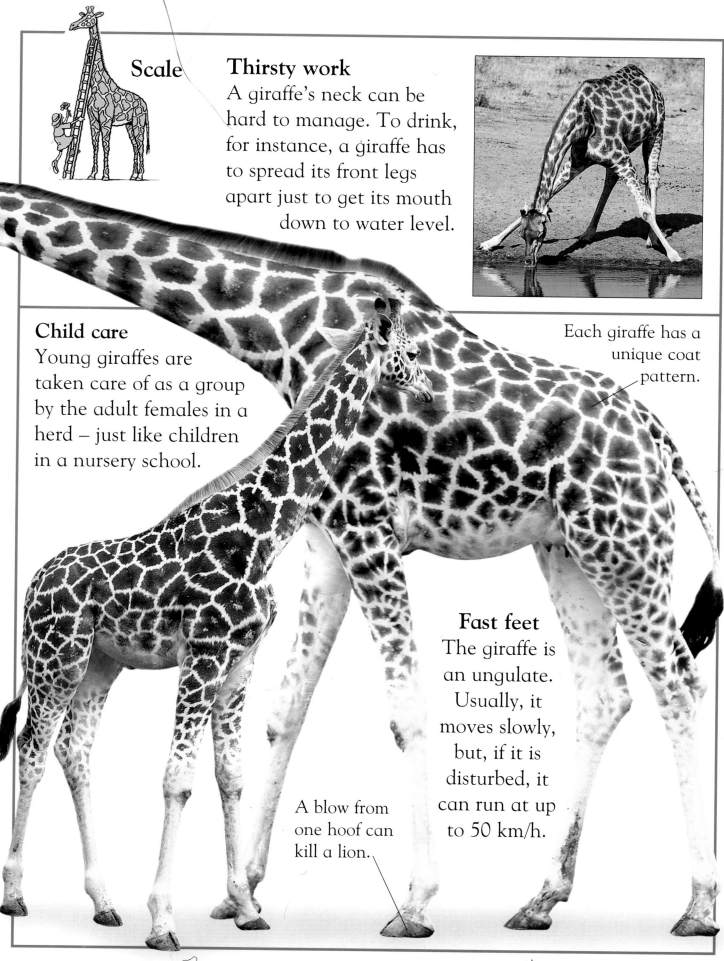

Scale

Thirsty work
A giraffe's neck can be hard to manage. To drink, for instance, a giraffe has to spread its front legs apart just to get its mouth down to water level.

Child care
Young giraffes are taken care of as a group by the adult females in a herd – just like children in a nursery school.

Each giraffe has a unique coat pattern.

Fast feet
The giraffe is an ungulate. Usually, it moves slowly, but, if it is disturbed, it can run at up to 50 km/h.

A blow from one hoof can kill a lion.

Ungulates are animals that have hoofs.

Rhinoceros

Black rhinos can be very aggressive. Sometimes they charge at speeds of up to 50 km/h for no apparent reason.

White rhinos, like the one above, have horns that can grow more than a metre long – that's at least twice the length of your arm.

Like other ungulates, rhinos do not use their heel bones for walking – so rhinos walk and run on their toes.

There are five species of rhino: the white and the black rhinos of Africa, and the Indian, Sumatran, and Javan rhinos. The largest is the white rhino, the second biggest animal on land. This armoured beast is an Indian rhino.

Indian rhinos have only one small horn.

Sense ability
All rhinos have poor eyesight and cannot see very far, but they have a very good sense of hearing and smell.

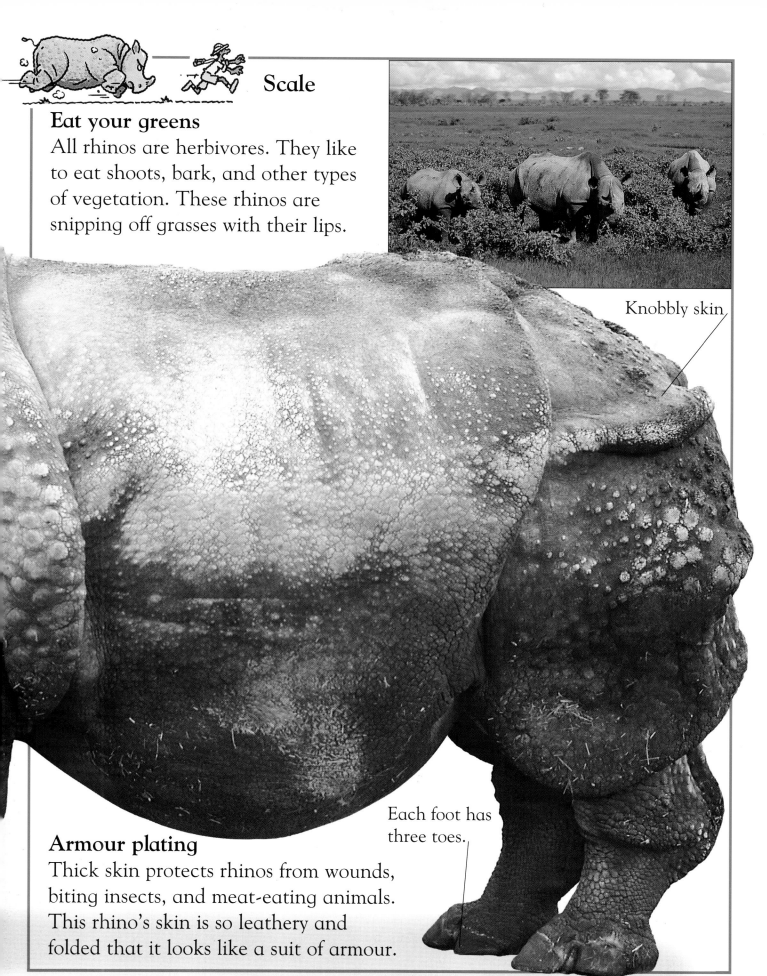

Scale

Eat your greens

All rhinos are herbivores. They like to eat shoots, bark, and other types of vegetation. These rhinos are snipping off grasses with their lips.

Knobbly skin

Armour plating

Thick skin protects rhinos from wounds, biting insects, and meat-eating animals. This rhino's skin is so leathery and folded that it looks like a suit of armour.

Each foot has three toes.